Kit VI

Critical Reading

Donald C. Cushenbery, Ed.D.
and
Ronald E. Meyer, M.S.

Reading Comprehension Mastery Kits

The Center for Applied Research in Education
West Nyack, New York 10994

ISBN: 0-13-030397-6

READING COMPREHENSION MASTERY KITS

KIT I   Understanding Details
KIT II   Recognizing Main Ideas
KIT III   Drawing Conclusions
KIT IV   Following Directions
KIT V   Locating Hidden Meaning
KIT VI   Critical Reading

Note: Each Kit includes 30 sequential lessons
for building ten specific subskills of a
major reading skill, complete answer keys
and a mastery test.

Adapted from READING COMPREHENSION MAS-
TERY KITS by Donald C. Cushenbery, Ed.D. and Ronald
E. Meyer, M.S. (West Nyack, NY: The Center for Applied
Research in Education, 1980).

Additional copies of this student workbook or any of the
other workbooks listed in the box above may be obtain-
ed from the publisher by calling 1-800-288-4745.

The Center for Applied Research in Education
West Nyack, New York 10994

To Help You Get Started

Did you ever think that what you read might not be true?

Sometimes we think that printed material cannot be wrong. The truth is that writing is often wrong. Sometimes important ideas are left out. Sometimes the things we read are so old that they are not right any more. Sometimes a writer wants to believe something so badly that he or she stretches the truth. Sometimes we read things by people who are not experts—they just do not know much about what they are writing.

We should be interested in how truthful an author's writing is, and we should also be interested in how well an author writes. Does he or she write clearly? Does the writing fit the message?

The lessons in this kit will help you think more about the author and writing. The "Technical Talk" section in each unit of lessons will give you some things you need to know. Then you will have the chance to use those things in the "Try It" sections. If you still have questions about lesson 1 in each unit, lesson 2 may help. It tells you how to think about the first lesson to get the right answer.

Be sure to read the directions carefully. After you have the directions in mind, go ahead and read the selection and complete the exercises. If you need help, be sure to speak with your teacher.

KEEPING RECORDS

You should keep records of how well you do in each unit of lessons. Records help you see progress. They also show when you need help in a skill. Your teacher may want to review your records after each unit.

Unit Records

At the end of each unit of lessons there is a section called "How Did You Do?" with a graph to help you keep a record of your correct answers. Here is how to use it:

1. Count the number of correct answers you had in the unit. Write this number in the top of the left-hand box next to "Number Correct." (See the sample below.) The number of possible correct answers in the unit is already printed in the bottom of this box next to "Possible."

2. Find the "Number Correct" above the bar graph.

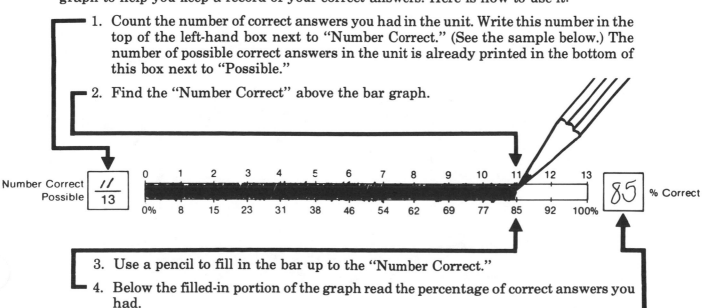

3. Use a pencil to fill in the bar up to the "Number Correct."

4. Below the filled-in portion of the graph read the percentage of correct answers you had.

5. Write the "Percentage Correct" in the right-hand box.

Score Sheet

You should also keep a record of how you do in all of the lesson units in this kit. There is a graph at the back of the kit to help. Here is how to use it:

1. When you finish Unit 1, use a pencil to fill in the bar for that unit on the score sheet. The numbers above the bar are percentages. The filled-in portion of the bar tells you the percentage of correct answers you had for that unit.

2. When you are finished with all of the units, you will be able to compare the bars to find out in which units you did best. You will also be able to find out in which units you need more practice.

SCORE SHEET

Kit VI   Critical Reading

STUDENT'S NAME: *Andy Martin*

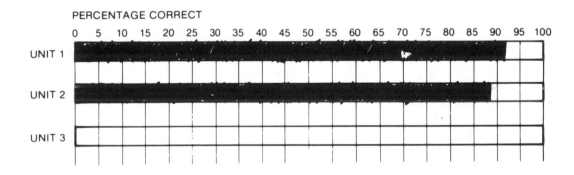

Table of Contents

Given the choice of several authors, the reader selects the one best qualified in a subject.

TECHNICAL TALK

Part of critical reading is finding the right author. There are some writers who know almost everything there is to know about something. But there are also people who know very little about their subject. That doesn't always keep them from writing.

For example, if you wanted to know about how high schools are run, which person would you ask?

A retired sea captain who has not been in school for 30 years.
A 17-year-old who has been in high school for two years.
An elementary school teacher.

You would probably ask the high school student. That is the person with the most information about the high school.

TRY IT

There are three subjects below and several authors. Match the best writer for each subject.

WHO CAN YOU TRUST?

Subject	Author
___ 1. The Civil War	(a) A man who was once President
___ 2. The Model T Ford	(b) Someone who rode trains for 30 years
___ 3. The White House	(c) A general who has studied the history of wars
	(d) A mechanic who owns antique cars
	(e) A policeman interested in art

If you picked (c) the general, (d) the mechanic, and (a) the ex-President, you are right. Each of these people has the experience he needs. Remember, the person who has experience or training will usually be more expert than the one who has none.

FIND THE EXPERT

Which of these authors wrote about a subject he or she knows about? Mark one box with an "X" to show which one is the expert.

1. ☐ Anne J. Arbuckle teaches at a college. She is a very good teacher, especially in American history. She likes people and helps them whenever she can. Dr. Arbuckle has many hobbies. She likes to ride horses, and she takes pictures. She reads a lot about the history of art. She wrote a book titled *The Cat as a House Pet.*

2. ☐ Jonathan R. Smisely loves old cars. His friends say he is the best mechanic they know. He can listen to a car for two minutes and tell what is wrong with it. John also collects old auto parts and pictures of cars. He wrote a book about the engines in jet planes.

3. ☐ Anne Jantzen is a high school student who likes to cook. She has lots of friends who come to her house just to hang around and talk. She learned a long time ago that parties are more fun if there is plenty to eat. She started cooking snacks for her friends. They think she does a great job. She does especially well on pizza and certain sandwiches. Carol wrote a book titled *Thirty Snacks for Drop-Ins.*

THE CIVIL WAR—WHO KNOWS?

All of the authors below plan to write about the same subject—the American Civil War. Each one has had special experiences that will help him or her write about a certain part of the war. Match the author with the two books each person might be best qualified to write.

(a) Jane Bouton had a great grandfather who was a boy during the Civil War. He used to tell her stories about how he grew up during the war years. She has been interested in those days all her life. She has read dozens of diaries and letters written by parents and friends to soldiers who fought in the war. She even has a collection of letters sent to soldiers by wives who stayed at home and waited for news.

(b) Earl Stanton has been interested for many years in Civil War battles. He owns an old cannon he believes was used in one battle. On his vacations, he visits the battlefields of the war and takes notes on the things he sees. He has even written to generals asking them about battles and how they were fought.

(c) James Stout is interested in medicine. He found out that "doctoring" during the Civil War was often crude and dangerous. The doctors had nothing to kill germs with in those days. Operations that are easy today often killed soldiers who were hurt. Arms and legs had to be cut off to save many men. Stout has studied the ways doctors worked.

_____ 1. A book about the weapons used in the Civil War.

_____ 2. A book about the kind of wounds caused by fighting.

_____ 3. A book about how the war affected children.

_____ 4. A book about the three longest battles fought in the Civil War.

_____ 5. A book about the number of men who died in Army hospitals.

_____ 6. A book about the problems people at home had in getting food during the Civil War.

HOW DID YOU DO?

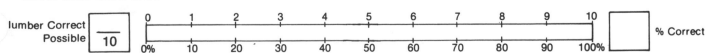

Number Correct Possible 10

% Correct

Given *Who's Who* or an encyclopedia as a reference, the reader selects the most appropriate author for a certain purpose.

UNIT 2
Lesson 1
Critical Reading

TECHNICAL TALK

Who's Who in America is a book you can find in most libraries. Each edition lists famous living people and information about them. If you hear the name of someone who seems to be famous, you can use *Who's Who* to find out about him or her. For example, if you want to find out about a well-known author, look for his or her name in *Who's Who*.

WHO KNOWS ABOUT PLANES?

Here are two listings like some in *Who's Who in America*. Which person would you choose as an author to write about airplanes?

JACKSON, DWIGHT, army officer, engineer; b. Springfield, Mass., June 19, 1784; attended Hanston College; leader in development of fast ships; commanded exploring groups, eastern New Mexico, 1818; best known for work on sailing ship design. Died, Boston, March 21, 1869.

GILMAN, EDGAR, engineer, aircraft designer; b. Chicago, Ill. July 1, 1900; attended University of Chicago; entered design work with Hansen Aircraft, 1927; became chief design engineer, 1939; leader in design of new airfoils during World War II; retired 1965. Died, Langston, Tex., 1973.

I would choose _____

If you picked Edgar Gilman you are right. Edgar Gilman was not a real person, but anyone with his experience would have been an expert on airplanes. When did Dwight Jackson die? In the last line of the statement about him it says he died in 1869. That was before airplanes were invented, so he could not have written about them.

EXPERT EXPLORERS

For this activity, you will need a copy of *Who's Who in America: The Historical Volume 1608-1896*. If you cannot find this book, try a good encyclopedia. You can find the information you need for the activity in the encyclopedia, too, though it will take a little longer.

Look up the name of each person in the following list. Find the two people who could write about exploring the early West. Write their names on the lines below.

Samuel Colt
John Jacob Astor
Frederick Douglass
John Colter

These are the two experts I picked:

1. _____

2. _____

WHO DID WHAT?

You will need an encyclopedia for this activity.

Look up the name of each of the following people in the encyclopedia and read the entry for him or her. Then put the letter in front of each person's name below to show in which field he or she is an expert.

(a) Maria Callas
(b) Al Capp
(c) William Kidd
(d) Lewis Carroll
(e) Shirley Chisholm
(f) Samuel Morse
(g) John Muir

Which one of the persons listed above would be expert in:

_____ 1. Paintings

_____ 2. Children's Books

_____ 3. Opera

_____ 4. Cartoons

_____ 5. Politics

_____ 6. Pirates

_____ 7. Conservation

HOW DID YOU DO?

Number Correct / Possible [10]

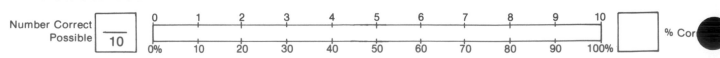

% Cor

Given two short paragraphs one of which takes a strong stand and the other of which provides information, the student discriminates between them.

TECHNICAL TALK

Can you tell when someone is pushing you? You can tell if someone is trying to push you out of a line. That's easy. But can you tell when someone is trying to push the way you think? A writer may try to do this by using writing tricks. One of these tricks is called <u>editorializing</u>.

TRY IT

One of the following paragraphs gives the author's feelings. The other does not. Can you tell which is which?

WRESTLING ALLIGATORS

(a) John Morgan wrestles alligators. He has spent many of the last 20 years flipping the beasts. He works in a park in Florida. People pay to see him jump into a pit and grab two animals at once. Each one is at least six feet long. He says he must be careful to stay away from their tails. They can slap a person hard enough to break a leg. John's work is really disgusting.

(b) Anne Morgan is John's wife. She doesn't care for alligators. She said just a few weeks ago that she had had enough of the beasts. She said she once worried about John. Now she thinks the alligators are safe. She tried to wrestle one of the animals once. She had no trouble pinning a little one. Since then she laughs when her husband jumps into the pit. "They are like kittens," she says.

Paragraph _____ presents the author's opinion in the sentence: _____

_____

If you said paragraph (a), you are right. The last sentence in the paragraph states the author's own feelings: "John's work is really disgusting." Although you may agree with the author, this sentence does not state a fact. It gives an opinion. Giving an opinion is all right in some kinds of writing. But readers must be able to tell a fact from an opinion. Otherwise they may be tricked into believing something that is not true.

Read each of the sentences below. Mark each one with <u>F</u> if it is a fact or with <u>O</u> if it is opinion.

FACT OR OPINION

—— 1. Everyone should be allowed to drive.

—— 2. Driving is easy.

—— 3. More than 80 million people have driver's licenses.

—— 4. In most states drivers must take a test before they are licensed.

—— 5. Motorcycle riders should wear helmets.

—— 6. In some states the law says motorcycle riders must wear helmets.

—— 7. Many drivers say they do not like people who don't dim their lights at night.

—— 8. According to law, drivers can lose their licenses for reckless driving.

Now read each paragraph below. Look for one sentence in each paragraph that gives the <u>author's</u> opinion. You will find one in each paragraph.

Abraham Lincoln was a tall, thin man. He often wore a tall stovepipe hat. Ⓐ People thought the hat made him look like a giant. A lot of people laughed at him. The newspapers of his time were full of cartoons about him. Ⓑ They called him ugly and ignorant. A little girl thought his face needed something. She told him he would look better if he grew a beard. Ⓒ He wore a beard from that time on. Ⓓ Abraham Lincoln may have been ugly, but he was the greatest President who ever lived.

1. Which sentence shows the author's opinion about Abraham Lincoln? _____

Ⓐ The greatest warrior who ever lived was Geronimo. He was a chief of the Apache Indians. In 1876 the Apaches were forced onto the White Mountain Reservation. Geronimo led his followers to camps in the mountains. Ⓑ They hid there and were safe. Ⓒ From those camps Geronimo led raids into Mexico and Arizona. For more than ten years he terrorized people near Tucson, Arizona. Ⓓ He was finally captured in 1866 and sent to Florida.

GERONIMO

2. Which sentence shows the author's opinion? _____

Ⓐ Clark Gable was born in Cadiz, Ohio, in 1901. Ⓑ He was the most handsome movie star of his time. His movies included *Mutiny on the Bounty* and *Gone with the Wind.* Ⓒ He started acting in Kansas City when he was 19. Before that he had worked in a rubber factory. People have called him one of the most famous movie stars who ever lived.

3. Which sentence shows the author's opinion? _____

HOW DID YOU DO?

mber Correct		0	1	2	3	4	5	6	7	8	9	10	11	12		% Correct
Possible	12	0%	8	17	25	33	42	50	58	67	75	83	92	100%		

Given a selection, the reader identifies it as either imagined or real.

UNIT 4
Lesson 1
Critical Reading

TECHNICAL TALK

Is an author telling you about a dream world or about the real thing? It is sometimes important to know the difference between the real and fantastic. We can learn a lot by reading fantasy, but we need to be able to separate it from the things that can really happen today.

TRY IT

Here are some famous stories. Read the descriptions and mark each one to show whether it could happen or not.

FAMOUS FANTASY

1. ☐ Could happen   *Gulliver's Travels* by Jonathan Swift
   ☐ Fantasy   A man named Gulliver goes to a foreign country. He goes to sleep on a seashore and wakes up with little people all around him. They have used little strings and stakes to tie him to the ground. He can't move.

2. ☐ Could happen   *Alice in Wonderland* by Lewis Carroll
   ☐ Fantasy   Alice goes on a picnic. After lunch she meets a rabbit with a watch. He is very late for a meeting. Alice falls down a rabbit hole and has an adventure of the strangest kind.

3. ☐ Could happen   *2001: A Space Odyssey* by Arthur C. Clarke
   ☐ Fantasy   A scientist leaves for the moon and finds a strange machine buried there. Later an astronaut fights with the computer on his spaceship. The computer has already killed all the people on the ship except him.

4. ☐ Could happen   *Animal Farm* by George Orwell
   ☐ Fantasy   A group of animals on a farm are ruled for a time by a pig who is a dictator.

5. ☐ Could happen   *20,000 Leagues Under the Sea* by Jules Verne
   ☐ Fantasy   A white-hot energy source drives a submarine through the sea for thousands of miles. The crew eats only sea animals and plants it gathers from fields on the ocean floor.

All the books listed in lesson 1 are famous fantasies. Each one has had some effect on what people think or feel about their lives and times. Fantasy is important to us. Authors can use it to help us understand our real lives better.

For each paragraph below, mark whether you think it comes from a real setting or a fantasy.

LIGHT AND DARK

The screen glowed with stars. They started way out there as pinpoints of light and then grew bigger and bigger until they flashed off the screen on one side or the other. The ship hummed quietly even though it was moving at more than ten times the speed of light. The captain sat in his chair waiting for a call from the last outpost in space. The colony on the planet Zantar had been silent too long.

1. ☐ Real   2. ☐ Fantasy

There were no lights. It was strange. There was not a single light anywhere, but he knew there were men all around him. He could hear the bump of guns going off miles away. Once in a while he heard someone whisper or sensed the movement of a rifle as it bumped almost silently against another piece of equipment. But most of all he was aware of the absolute, eternal darkness.

1. ☐ Real   2. ☐ Fantasy

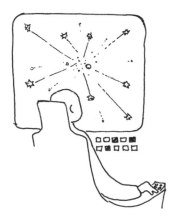

THREE STRANGE ONES

Here are descriptions of three characters in famous stories. See if you can tell by reading about each one whether he or she comes from a real or fantasy setting.

He was mixed up at first. He tried to move, but he couldn't. Chains held his arms and legs. Somehow he knew he was different than before. He could tell he was in a castle and there was equipment all around him. Most of it was electrical machinery he had never seen before. There were wires leading to buttons that were fixed to his neck. By turning his head just a little he could see part of the name on one of the machines. The letters were F-R-A-N-K-E-N-S-T- . . . .

1. ☐ Real   2. ☐ Fantasy

She opened the door just a crack to look in. What a strange appearance her grandmother had. She was lying in bed with the covers pulled up to her chin. She was wearing her glasses as usual, and she had that funny old sleeping cap on her head. But she seemed gray, and her nose was so long and strange. Her grandmother was awake, so she decided to go right in. She took off her red cape, picked up the picnic basket, and pushed open the door. Then grandmother smiled, revealing huge teeth she had never had before.

1. ☐ Real   2. ☐ Fantasy

He watched the lightning rip across the sky. At every flash he could see the string leading into the sky. The kite pulled violently against the silk line he held. He knew he was right. Electricity and lightning had to be the same thing. If he were right the sparks would run down the string. Electricity would get to the key, and jump to the jar. Then a sudden flash and bang lit up everything as lightning flashed near the kite. Ben watched the blue sparks jump from the key. He was right!

1. ☐ Real   2. ☐ Fantasy

HOW DID YOU DO?

Number Correct
Possible 10

0	1	2	3	4	5	6	7	8	9	10
0%	10	20	30	40	50	60	70	80	90	100%

% Corr

Given a selection, the student correctly interprets the mood.

TECHNICAL TALK

When an author writes he or she tries to tell us something. We get ideas from what we read. Many authors try to change our feelings about something, too. They might try to make us happy or angry or afraid. They create a mood that we react to. We may get the same feelings the author builds in his or her writing. It takes a good writer to create moods in us. When a writer is able to do this, we know that he or she is an artist.

TRY IT

The selection which follows tries to develop one of these moods: loneliness, anger, fear, happiness, hopelessness. Read it and decide which one of these moods the author wants you to feel.

MORNING WINDOW

Andyce looked out the window over the countryside. There seemed to be no sound at all. More than a mile away she could see farmer Tangdow walking beside his oxen and a load of hay, but his wagon made not a sound she could hear. Even the birds were quiet. The sky was a dull gray quilt, spread over the whole earth.

She watched the farmer and his cart. She was affected by the slowness of their movement. She couldn't see the road they moved along, but she measured their snail's pace against the trees they passed. She brushed her hair carefully and slowly as she watched. There seemed to be nothing else moving in the world but the farmer there and her.

What mood is the author trying to create?   (a) anger   (b) fear   (c) loneliness
(d) happiness   (e) hopelessness

The mood in the first selection was one of solitude or loneliness. Did you notice the images the author used? Did you try to picture and listen to what the author wrote about? There was no one else about. The sky was overcast. The only contact Andyce had with anyone was with the farmer who was so far away that she was still alone. The author helps us feel how Andyce felt. He has created a mood for us.

What mood do you sense in this next piece?

HAWK

The rabbit had seen the hawk high above, her black wings spread against the sun. The rabbit cocked his head and watched the hawk glide in wide circles. He sensed she was hungry and hunting. He crouched lower in the grass keeping still. He shivered a little as a breeze caught the fur on his side and moved it in little ripples.

Then he saw the hawk twist, fold its wings and begin a long dive straight at him. She put her feet first with those long claws down and pointed. She hurtled down with tremendous speed. The rabbit jumped sideways and took three long leaps, each in a different direction. The hawk's wings moved just a little first this way then that. She kept on target. Like an explosive charge she hit the rabbit. Fur and feathers flew, and blood marked the snowy ground. The hawk preened her feathers once with her razor-sharp bill and settled down to breakfast.

Mark the statement below that best describes the mood of this piece.

a. ☐   The author wants you to feel afraid for the rabbit.

b. ☐   The author wants you to see the violence of the kill. He does not feel sorry for the rabbit though.

c. ☐   The author wants you to be on the hawk's side.

Discuss your answer with others. Explain why you answered the way you did.

DRAGON FIGHT

There are two different moods in the following paragraphs. Read the paragraphs then select the sentence which best describes the mood in each one. Write the letter of the sentence you pick for each paragraph in the box at the beginning of the paragraph.

1. ☐ The dragon thrashed his tail. George could hear the beast's teeth grind and its breath burn the grass. Each time the dragon's tail or foot smashed into the ground the trees rocked. The roar the beast made was like thunder. George could see the soft, pale green belly of the huge animal. That's where the spear must strike. It was only there that the dragon could be killed. George bent over the spear. Its red streamer followed the wind as he leveled the weapon. He spurred his horse and yelled as they thundered down on the monster.

2. ☐ The stream gurgled peacefully under the bridge. Carrie looked deep into the water for one of the long brown trout. She often saw them there swimming sleepily near the rocks in the stream bed. The pine trees whispered in the wind. A bird chirped quietly in a nearby bush, but those were the only sounds. She needed a chance to think. This was the place for it.

(a) The mood is happy excitement.
(b) The mood is noisy and dangerous.
(c) The mood is bitter. The character feels beat, defeated.
(d) The mood is grey and miserable.
(e) Peace, solitude, and aloneness describe the mood.

HOW DID YOU DO?

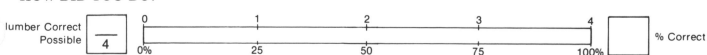

lumber Correct
Possible ☐ 4

0   1   2   3   4
0%   25   50   75   100%

% Correct ☐

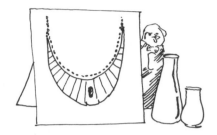

TECHNICAL TALK

Picture yourself walking in a museum full of treasures. It is pitch dark. You can't see a thing, but you know the rooms are full of rich and beautiful things. There are golden necklaces from Egypt. Hanging on the walls are paintings made by hundreds of the greatest artists who ever lived. There are tiny statues carved two thousand years ago by Romans. But it is so dark you can't see anything.

Turn on the lights! Being in a dark museum is just about like starting a new book. Great writers are able to paint pictures for us with words. They make "images" by telling us what they see, or hear, or taste, or feel in their own mind's eye. Good readers are able to follow the author's images or pictures and see them in their own minds.

TRY IT

Here is a description of a place. It has visual images and some sound pictures, too. Can you picture the surroundings and guess where you are?

SWALLOWED

The click-click-clickety-click went on as it had for hours. The only difference was the sudden darkness. I reached up and touched the window by my shoulder to make sure it was still there. Just seconds ago I could look out on the green and gold farm flashing by in the sun. "Swallowed by a dragon," I thought. The whole car—seats, people, me—gulped down in one bite. We were sliding down the inside of the dragon's throat. Would we ever get out again? Then suddenly light flashed through the window once more. We were through the . . . .

Describe what has happened: _____

_____

_____

_____

REVIEW

People could have different answers. The author was thinking about riding a fast train through a tunnel. The clicking sound, the farms flashing by, the car, seats and people—they all add up to high-speed travel. The sudden darkness comes when the train enters a tunnel.

Try another experiment. This time read the paragraphs below. For each sentence that begins with a circled letter, decide what kind of image the author is giving. Write the letter next to the image below.

FEAST

Ⓐ She sat at the table alone listening to the others eat. The noise of the silverware aginst dishes was almost like bells. She couldn't hear what people were saying, but their voices were happy. Ⓑ She could read their happiness in the buzz of talk. It was like bees almost. Bees that had plenty of honey.

Ⓒ The whole restaurant was crowded with people. The colors of their clothes made the room look like a patchwork quilt.

Ⓓ Each table had a candle in one of those little glass holders. The candles made a tiny golden halo on each table where the light danced slowly on the tablecloth.

Ⓔ But the smells captured her attention most. They took her back to her mother's kitchen. She tasted in her memory a hundred dinners she had eaten—turkeys at Thanksgiving, duck and steak and salads with savory dressings. They all came back as she sniffed the beautiful steam that came through the kitchen door. The smells were a feast themselves.

1. Visual images _____

2. Sound images _____

3. Smell images _____

4. Where does this event happen?   (a) in a friend's home   (b) in a restaurant   (c) at a Thanksgiving feast

Read this description. Then answer the questions about it. Pay special attention to the images the author uses.

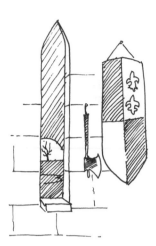

The sky was just beginning to lighten. At first, he could see only the window outlined against the sky. Then the sky was tinted by the rising sun. The stars disappeared, and he could see the walls of his room. Though he didn't want to get up, he swung his legs out of bed and placed his feet on the cold stone floor. Already he could smell the cooking below in the big dining halls of the castle. The cooks were making a big breakfast to carry them through the battle. He walked over to the bearskin rug and dressed quickly, hoping to warm up. He kept his feet on the rug as long as he could.

He whistled loudly and the sound echoed from the walls and down the halls. His squire came into the room from his cot outside the door. Together they began strapping on the lightest pieces of his armor. The sky was bright enough now that they could just see to fasten the buckles. Today would tell who would sleep here tomorrow.

1. The author is telling about a man getting ready for   (a) breakfast   (b) battle   (c) bed

2. This event happens   (a) early in the morning   (b) in a castle   (c) before a battle is fought   (d) all of the above

3. The author uses many images to set the scene. Which ones do you find? (a) sense of touch   (b) sight   (c) sound   (d) smell   (e) taste

HOW DID YOU DO?

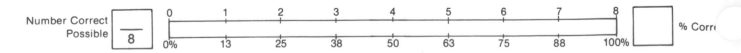

Number Correct
Possible   8

Number Correct | 0   1   2   3   4   5   6   7   8
0%   13   25   38   50   63   75   88   100%

% Corr

Given a paragraph, the reader identifies words that carry emotional impact.

TECHNICAL TALK

Authors use words with care. They know that certain words affect people strongly. If a writer wants you to become angry about something, he or she will use words that bring angry thoughts to mind. If he wants you to feel good about something, the writer will use pleasant words. Look at this example:

    1. His room was in a state of complete disorder.
    2. His room was just a messy pigpen.

See the difference? Sentence 1 makes a real mess sound pretty good. Sentence 2 makes a bad situation a lot worse than it really is.

TRY IT

Read the following paragraph and notice the words that are used to anger the reader.

TEENS ARE TERRIBLE

Teenagers are sometimes sloppy people. They leave their junk lying around wherever they happen to drop it. You can expect a trail of moldy socks, sticky pop cans, and smelly pizza boxes to follow them everywhere. They never hang up their clothes. They throw piles of rotting sneakers and other disgusting things in dark corners to mold. It's all a respectable person can do to live around these slobs.

Who would ever write such a thing? You can see hate hiding behind many of the underlined words. Check the words below that were used to make you believe teenagers are terrible.

1.	☐ teenagers	9.	☐ hang
2.	☐ sloppy	10.	☐ clothes
3.	☐ junk	11.	☐ piles
4.	☐ happen	12.	☐ rotting
5.	☐ sticky	13.	☐ mold
6.	☐ smelly	14.	☐ respectable
7.	☐ boxes	15.	☐ person
8.	☐ follow	16.	☐ slobs

Words that cause emotions in people are sometimes called "loaded words." In the paragraph about teenagers, the most loaded words are probably <u>sloppy</u>, <u>junk</u>, <u>sticky</u>, <u>smelly</u>, <u>piles</u>, <u>rotting</u>, <u>mold</u>, and <u>slobs</u>. If you changed these words you could make the whole paragraph more <u>honest</u>. Sometimes <u>authors</u> use words like this to get you stirred up. Loaded words are traps for people who do not take time to examine the facts and think.

Read the newscast below. Then pick one of the words or phrases below the paragraph to replace each numbered word. Select words or phrases to make the newscast more factual and less emotional.

RIP OFF!

Washington announced today that more money will be ①<u>thrown down an old rat hole.</u> ②<u>Bureaucrats</u> there are planning now to ③<u>throw away</u> another 15 million dollars to make our lives safer. They are planning to put new signs up on narrow bridges at ④<u>gigantic</u> cost to taxpayers. They have been ⑤<u>wasting</u> money on these ⑥<u>useless</u> signs for three years. The ⑦<u>big spenders</u> say they will finish the project next year.

Select less loaded words for each of the underlined words and phrases in the paragraph.

1. ☐ (a) wasted on a useless project   (or)   ☐ (b) spent on an old project
2. ☐ (a) Officials   (or)   ☐ (b) Big spenders
3. ☐ (a) waste   (or)   ☐ (b) spend
4. ☐ (a) substantial   (or)   ☐ (b) huge
5. ☐ (a) spending   (or)   ☐ (b) throwing away
6. ☐ (a) unneeded   (or)   ☐ (b) no good
7. ☐ (a) officials   (or)   ☐ (b) bureaucrats

Now read the paragraph again with the new words. See the difference word selection can make?

GREAT PILOT AWES WATCHERS

The paragraphs below can be written two ways just by using different words in the blank spaces. You will find two word choices for each blank in the two columns below the paragraphs. Pick words for the first paragraph to make the dog look like a hero. Then fill the blanks in the second paragraph with the unused words. The second paragraph should make the whole event seem completely different.

DOG FLIES OWN HOUSE

Today the ①_____ dog of comic fame flew his ②_____ doghouse over Metropolis. Acting as ③_____ as usual, he took off from the local airport, wearing his ④_____ flying cap and goggles. His ⑤_____ _____ scarf trailing behind, the little critter zoomed ⑥_____ over the city as thousands of people watched. After an hour of the ⑦_____ flying demonstration, the ⑧_____ returned to earth. The mayor met him on the ground to offer some ⑨_____ remarks about his performance.

Today the ①_____ dog of comic fame flew his ②_____ doghouse over Metropolis. Acting as ③_____ as usual, he took off from the local airport, wearing his ④_____ flying cap and goggles. His ⑤_____ _____ scarf trailing behind, the little critter zoomed ⑥_____ over the city as thousands of people watched. After an hour of the ⑦_____ flying demonstration, the ⑧_____ returned to earth. The mayor met him on the ground to offer some ⑨_____ remarks about his performance.

1.	heroic	(or)	black and white
2.	red-roofed	(or)	famed
3.	gallant	(or)	odd
4.	stupid looking	(or)	famous
5.	romantic	(or)	floppy
6.	wildly	(or)	daringly
7.	dangerous	(or)	unusual
8.	mutt	(or)	dog
9.	glowing	(or)	angry

HOW DID YOU DO?

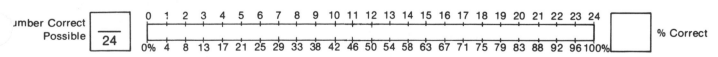

umber Correct
Possible 24

0 1 2 3 4 5 6 7 8 9 10 11 12 13 14 15 16 17 18 19 20 21 22 23 24

0% 4 8 13 17 21 25 29 33 38 42 46 50 54 58 63 67 71 75 79 83 88 92 96 100%

% Correct

Given a selection in which an author is trying to get one to do something, the reader selects the best statement about the author's intent.

UNIT 8
Lesson 1
Critical Reading

TECHNICAL TALK

Some people write to get you to do something. American history is full of examples of writing that helped change the way people thought. In 1852, Harriet Beecher Stowe wrote a book called *Uncle Tom's Cabin* about people caught in slavery. The book made readers think about slavery. Hundreds of thousands of people read it. When President Abraham Lincoln met Mrs. Stowe, he called her the little woman who started a great war. Of course a lot of other things helped cause the Civil War, but Mrs. Stowe's book was one powerful influence.

TRY IT

The paragraph below was written during the American Revolution by Thomas Paine. It was bitter cold at Valley Forge. The soldiers were freezing and hungry. George Washington asked Paine to write something to fire up his men and keep their spirits up. Read the paragraph carefully. Then mark the statement below that best tells what Thomas Paine was asking for.

STAND WITH US!

... I turn with the warm ardor of a friend to those who have nobly stood, and are yet determined to stand the matter out: I call not upon a few, but upon all; not on <u>this</u> state or <u>that</u> state, but on <u>every</u> state; up and help us; lay your shoulders to the wheel; better have too much force than too little, when so great an object is at stake. Let it be told to the future world, that in the depth of winter, when nothing but hope and virtue could survive, that the city and the country, alarmed at one common danger, came forth to meet and repulse it.

Thomas Paine wants you to

(a) ☐ Keep out of trouble any way you can.

(b) ☐ Join with the soldiers so they can overcome the danger they are in.

(c) ☐ Pay more taxes so there will be enough food for the men.

(d) ☐ Worry less about the soldiers. They will win the battles they fight.

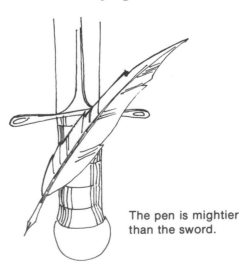

The pen is mightier than the sword.

Thomas Paine was a famous writer during the days of the American revolution. He is sometimes called the grandfather of America. He wrote books and pamphlets. The pamphlets were short articles to get people excited. They worked. They did excite people about fighting the Revolutionary War. Some of Thomas Paine's writings helped move the colonists to rebel. They may have made an important contribution to our winning the war against England. (b) is the right answer to lesson 1.

Here are some slogans. Slogans are short, catchy sayings used to get people to do things. Sometimes pictures are used with the slogans. Match each slogan with the best statement about what the writer wants you to do.

SLOGANS

____ 1. Be prepared.

____ 2. Uncle Sam wants you!

____ 3. Fly the friendly skies.

____ 4. A penny saved is a penny earned.

____ 5. Haste makes waste.

____ 6. Right wrongs no man.

____ 7. Many hands make light work.

(a) This slogan was used to get people to sign up for the army.

(b) This slogan tried to get people to ride on one of the major airlines.

(c) Slow down and do your work carefully.

(d) Help other people with their work and it will be easier for everyone.

(e) This famous slogan has asked millions of boys to be ready for anything.

(f) Always do the right thing and nobody will be hurt.

(g) Benjamin Franklin wrote this one. It means save your money and you will have it.

Each of the following short paragraphs is part of an advertisement that wants you to do something. Where might you find each one? Choose an answer for each paragraph.

____ 1. Get the highest interest for your money. No bank offers more. First Federal Savings and Loan Association offers 7½% interest. Put your money where it counts!

____ 2. Get into the Starflame 6. Your first feeling is room. There is more space than you have ever had before. The front seat leaves room for the passenger to relax. Space is the key.

____ 3. Here's the chance to do all your shopping from your own home! You'll find gifts for every event—from birthdays to Christmas. Pick the perfect gifts for your family and friends. Easy payment plan. Send in your order, now!

____ 4. Having trouble remembering? Improve your memory instantly with Dr. Arthur J. Fieldmore's exciting new book. It gives you 40 simple ways to remember facts, faces, anything. Don't forget. Order today!

(a) This is part of an ad in a magazine. Its purpose is to get the reader to buy a book.

(b) This could be part of a sales booklet about a car.

(c) You might see this in a pamphlet you could find at a savings company.

(d) This is the first paragraph of a mail order catalog.

HOW DID YOU DO?

Number Correct / Possible: 12

0	1	2	3	4	5	6	7	8	9	10	11	12
0%	8	17	25	33	42	50	58	67	75	83	92	100%

% Co

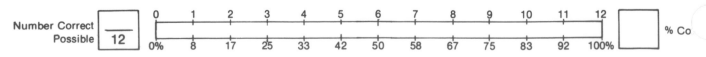

Given a simile, the reader identifies its literal meaning.

TECHNICAL TALK

A good writer uses things the reader knows. The writer wants you to understand exactly what he or she wants to say. Sometimes <u>figures</u> <u>of</u> <u>speech</u> are used this way. You may have heard Superman's introduction. Remember? "Faster than a speeding bullet, more powerful than a locomotive..." We all know how fast bullets move and if you have ever stood by a railroad track when a train rushed by, you have felt the power it has. This unit deals with some figures of speech.

TRY IT

A <u>simile</u> is a figure of speech. It helps you understand something by comparing it to something else. Below are several similes you may have heard. See if you can put the sentences back together. Write the letter in the line for each number.

FAMOUS "LIKES"

___ 1. That shook when he laughed ...

(a) like an old coat, all tattered and torn.

___ 2. Up above the world so high ...

(b) like a red, red rose.

___ 3. It was as black ...

(c) as midnight.

___ 4. The dawn comes up ...

(d) like a bowl full of jelly.

___ 5. My love is ...

(e) like a diamond in the sky.

___ 6. Once I was happy, but now I'm forlorn, ...

(f) like thunder out across the bay.

A simile compares one thing to another. Almost all similes have the words "like" or "as" in them. Each of the similes in the last lesson comes from a poem or song or an old saying. Did you get them all? Check your answers with the answer key.

Look for similes, they help us understand the writer's ideas. Here are some more. See if you can match these.

SAYINGS

___	1. swift	(a)	than greased lightning
___	2. green	(b)	as a hornet
___	3. high	(c)	as a snake's belly
___	4. quick	(d)	as a kite
___	5. smooth	(e)	as an eagle
___	6. sweet	(f)	as honey
___	7. faster	(g)	as a newborn babe
___	8. mad	(h)	as a whistle
___	9. innocent	(i)	as grass
___	10. dirty	(j)	as silk
___	11. low	(k)	as a pig
___	12. happy	(l)	as a lark
___	13. pretty	(m)	as a picture
___	14. straight	(n)	as a wink
___	15. clean	(o)	as an arrow

Some of these are very old sayings. People use them in talking, but you will not see them very much in writing. Why? They are so old that they have been used too much. Writers try to think up new comparisons to make similes. You should think up new ones, too. These are worn out like old socks.

Read the paragraphs below. Match the sayings about guns to what you think the meaning is for each one.

LOCK, STOCK, AND BARREL

Figures of speech, or "sayings" as some people call them, come from everyday things. During the pioneer days in America guns were as important as cars are today. Most families had guns for hunting and protection. Sometimes men even carried guns to church during troubled times. It was natural then for people to compare things to their guns. It helped them to better explain their ideas.

Guns then were complicated to use. They had to be loaded carefully. In very early times the gun was fired when flint hit against steel. The sparks this caused dropped into a little pan full of gunpowder. The powder burned down through a little hole into the gun barrel. There it set off the powder that drove the bullet. If the powder did not burn through the hole, the gun did not fire. When that happened people called it a "flash in the pan." Sometimes they used those same words to describe a person who succeeded brilliantly once but never again.

Try matching these other figures of speech about guns with their meanings. Use a dictionary if you need to. Look up the underlined words.

____ 1. He stood straight as a <u>ramrod</u>.

____ 2. The whole project <u>misfired</u>.

____ 3. Mrs. Brody lost her belongings <u>lock</u>, <u>stock</u>, and <u>barrel</u>.

(a) He stood very relaxed and on one leg.

(b) The project blew up.

(c) He stood with his back perfectly straight.

(d) Mrs. Brody lost a door lock, some cows, and a barrel of something.

(e) Nothing happened in the project when it was supposed to.

(f) Mrs. Brody lost everything she owned.

HOW DID YOU DO?

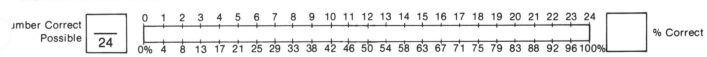

umber Correct Possible | 24 | 0 1 2 3 4 5 6 7 8 9 10 11 12 13 14 15 16 17 18 19 20 21 22 23 24   % Correct
0% 4 8 13 17 21 25 29 33 38 42 46 50 54 58 63 67 71 75 79 83 88 92 96 100%

Given a selection, the student discusses a few characteristics of the author's style.

UNIT 10
Lesson 1
Critical Reading

TECHNICAL TALK

Authors have different styles of writing. One author may use very short sentences. Another may use long, involved sentences. One author may use short, common words; another may use longer or more unusual words. Some authors use a lot of images and figures of speech while others use mainly description. Many of the lessons in this kit discuss the things an author can include to develop a special style. Let's put some of these things together and compare the style in several short paragraphs.

TRY IT

Read the paragraph below. Then answer the questions.

CAPYBARA

(A) Have you ever heard of the capybara? (B) It is an animal that lives in South America. (C) It is the largest of all rodents, so it is a cousin of rats, squirrels, and beavers. (D) How big is the capybara? (E) It grows to be four feet long and weighs in at more than 100 pounds. (F) It looks something like a small pig with stiff brown or gray hair. (G) The capybara is a good swimmer. (H) In fact, it has webbed toes and likes to stay around water. (I) People sometimes call the capybara a "water hog."

1. Which sentence is the longest one? ____

2. Which sentence is the shortest? ____

3. How many words in the paragraph have three or more syllables? ____

4. How many questions are asked? ____

5. What comparison does the writer use to help you understand what a capybara looks like? ____

_____

6. Do you think the style of the author is easy to read? _____

In the piece about capybaras the longest sentence is Ⓒ. It has 17 words. The shortest sentence is Ⓓ with 5 words. Sentence length is one key to style. The average sentence length for this paragraph is a little more than 10 words. Generally it is easier to read short sentences than long ones.

Words are also important. There are six words that have three syllables or more. The author's style depends partly on the length and strangeness of words used. Considering everything, the paragraph about capybaras is fairly easy to read. Read the next two paragraphs. Decide which is easier to read and tell why.

MAYAN POTTERY

THE MAYAS

① The Maya Indians onced lived in Central America. They built cities but did not live in them. The Mayan people lived in scattered huts. On their small farms they grew and ate corn, beans, squash, and chili peppers. They ate little meat because they kept only dogs and turkeys. When the Mayas had a celebration they went to a city. There they danced, sang, held religious events, and sometimes offered human sacrifices. As soon as the celebration was over, they went back home to their farms. The city was deserted once again.

② Mayan art was often used for religious purposes. The artists painted temple walls with large colorful murals that had no shadows or perspective in them. Sculptors chiseled small statues and very complicated pillars of symbols related to the gods they worshipped. Artists also decorated everyday things like pottery with paintings, and these sometimes showed everyday scenes that were less likely to have religious importance.

Which paragraph is more difficult? Explain your answer by comparing word lengths, sentence lengths, and the difficulty of words the author uses.

_____

_____

_____

_____

_____

_____

KNIGHTS IN SHINING ARMOR

Read this article about knights. It includes some unusual words that make for difficult reading. Look up each word in a dictionary and write its meaning below.

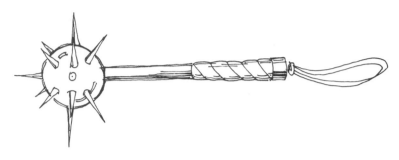

Knights were highly trained warriors who <u>flourished</u> in the years from about 1100 to 1500 A.D. We could compare them to army officers today. They were trained to fight with all kinds of weapons. They might use swords, battle axes, <u>lances</u>, or <u>maces</u> in battle. Knights wore heavy armor to protect their bodies. Before 1300, knights wore <u>conical</u> helmets to protect their heads and noses. Padded jackets and <u>mail</u> protected the body. In later years the knights wore heavy steel armor. It included many parts that were buckled onto the man's body. <u>Gauntlets</u> covered the hands and <u>sollerets</u> the feet.

When guns came into use, the armor was made so heavy that a crane had to be used to put a knight on his horse. If he fell off his horse, he could not even get up off the ground. Of course, the horses had to be very big and strong. They had to carry the knight, his armor, and the horse's armor, too.

Look up these words and write their meanings.

1. flourished _____

2. lance _____

3. mace _____

4. conical _____

5. mail (the armor kind) _____

6. gauntlet _____

7. solleret _____

Now read the paragraph again. Notice how much better you can understand the full meaning when you know the words. When you read, make a habit of using your dictionary to look up words you don't know.

HOW DID YOU DO?

Number Correct		0	1	2	3	4	5	6	7	8	9	10	11	12	13	14		% C(
Possible	14	0%	7	14	21	29	36	43	50	57	64	71	79	86	93	100%		

Answer Keys for Kit VI— *Critical Reading*

Unit 1

Lesson 1
1. c. general
2. d. mechanic
3. a. ex-President

Lesson 2
No. 3, Anne Jantzen, is the best choice.

Lesson 3
1. b
2. c
3. a
4. b
5. c
6. a

Unit 2

Lesson 1
Edgar Gilman

Lesson 2
1. John Jacob Astor
2. John Colter

Lesson 3
1. (f) Samuel Morse
2. (d) Lewis Carroll
3. (a) Maria Callas
4. (b) Al Capp
5. (e) Shirley Chisholm
6. (c) William Kidd
7. (g) John Muir

Unit 3

Lesson 1
Paragraph (a) presents the author's opinion in the sentence "John's work is really disgusting."

Lesson 2
1. O
2. O
3. F
4. F
5. O
6. F
7. F
8. F

Lesson 3
1. D
2. A
3. B

Unit 4

Lesson 1
1. Fantasy
2. Fantasy
3. Fantasy
4. Fantasy
5. Fantasy

Lesson 2
1. Fantasy
2. Real

Lesson 3
1. Fantasy
2. Fantasy
3. Real

Unit 5

Lesson 1
c. loneliness

Lesson 2
b. The author wants you to see the violence but not to feel sorry for the rabbit. He never discusses the rabbit's feelings or, for that matter, the hawk's. If he had wanted to create a mood of fear, he would have described the fear.

Lesson 3
1. b
2. e

Unit 6

Lesson 1
The person who is telling the story is traveling through a railroad tunnel on a train.

Lesson 2
1. C and D
2. A and B
3. E
4. b

Lesson 3
1. b
2. d
3. a, b, c, and d

Unit 7

Lesson 1
Correct answers are 2, 3, 5, 6, 11, 12, 13, and 16.

Lesson 2
1. b
2. a
3. b
4. a
5. a
6. a
7. a

Lesson 3
The dog as a hero:
1. heroic
2. famed
3. gallant
4. famous
5. romantic
6. daringly
7. unusual
8. dog
9. glowing

The dog as a common menace:
  black and white
  red-roofed
  odd
  stupid looking
  floppy
  wildly
  dangerous
  mutt
  angry

Unit 8

Lesson 1   b

Lesson 2   1. e
            2. a
            3. b
            4. g
            5. c
            6. f
            7. d

Lesson 3   1. c
            2. b
            3. d
            4. a

Unit 9

Lesson 1   1. d
            2. e
            3. c
            4. f
            5. b
            6. a

Lesson 2   1. e
            2. i
            3. d

            4. n
            5. j
            6. f
            7. a
            8. b
            9. g
           10. k
           11. c
           12. l
           13. m
           14. o
           15. h

Lesson 3   1. c
            2. e
            3. f

Unit 10

Lesson 1   1. C
            2. D
            3. 6
            4. 2
            5. "It looks something like a small pig."
            6. Yes or fairly easy

Lesson 2   Paragraph 1 is the easier of the two. The sentences are shorter and less complex. The words used in the second paragraph are more specialized and unfamiliar.

Lesson 3   1. were successful, were at their peak
            2. a spear-like weapon with a metal head
            3. a club with metal spikes
            4. cone-shaped
            5. interlinking metal rings
            6. a metal glove with a cuff
            7. armor for the foot

Mastery Test in Critical Reading

Name _____ *Date* _____

You have now finished all of the ten units in *Critical Reading*. You have worked with ten different skills. We want to see if you can use all of these skills in taking this test. When your test is scored, you will be able to see how much you have learned from the lessons.

Directions: Read all of the selections in this test carefully and answer the questions that follow them. You can check your progress by looking at the section "How Did You Do?" following the last question.

I.   WHO WILL YOU TRUST?

(a) Jessie Anderson is in prison. He was sentenced to five years for armed robbery after he held up a grocery store. He has spent four of the years in prison studying. When he gets out next year he plans to go to college and become an engineer. He isn't interested in more robberies or more time in jail.

(b) Anne Benton is a model. She has had her picture in five different magazines. She usually models sportswear and makeup. Anne thinks modelling is hard work, but she likes it. She spends some of her time on hobbies, including hang gliding and skiing. She is also interested in photography but is just starting that.

(c) Marty Jensen is a photographer. She spent four years studying art and then another two in photography school. She is especially interested in close-up work with plants and animals. Marty made her cat famous by photographing him for the cover of a pet magazine. Marty has done well in her work and now lives in an expensive apartment in New York.

1. Who could best write about makeup for teenagers? _____

2. Who probably knows most about courtrooms? _____

3. Who could write best about different film for taking pictures? _____

4. Who could write about the problems of prison? _____

5. Who might know most about artists of the 15th century? _____

II.   MONSTERS WE HAVE KNOWN AND LOVED

①People have always been interested in monsters.② There are books, movies, and comics about them.③ Two that have become popular are Frankenstein's monster and Dracula.④ Frankenstein's monster comes from a book by Mary Shelley who wrote about him in the 1800's. ⑤ Then several films were made about the Frankenstein monster in the 1930's. ⑥ No matter what happened to him at the end of one film, he was always revived for the next one.⑦ People liked Frankenstein movies because they wanted to have the great strength of the monster themselves.

There are two sentences in this paragraph that give opinions. Write the two sentences below.

6. _____

7. _____

III.   WAGONS

The sky blazed with red and gold. Sunset on the prairie was usually bright and cheerful. The long line of wagons ahead was just visible through the dust they raised. Their slow, plodding movement hardly seemed fast enough to take them across the great land, but each day they were a little closer to the mountains and their new home.

8. Should this selection be classed as a fantasy? _____

9. The description used mostly   (a) visual images   (b) sound images

10. The best description of the mood is   (a) hopeful   (b) sad

                                           MESSENGER

The sound filled his whole mind. It started like a groan then turned slowly into a scream. He knew it was the last step of his long, long trip. The heavy air of the new planet was clawing at the outside of the ship. He raised his arm heavily and pushed the computer command buttons. He pictured the landing step by step. Then he thought of the news he had to give the new world pioneers. The sound quieted to a whisper as he felt the anti-grav landers take over. He wished there were a better message.

11. Should this selection be classed as a fantasy? _____

12. The description uses mostly   (a) visual images   (b) sound images

13. The best description of the mood is   (a) cheerful   (b) fearful

IV.   LOOSE DOGS

There is a law in this city that all dogs must be tied up! This law was passed to protect innocent people from   (a) vicious   (b) stray   dogs. There are enough dangers for our children. We don't need   (a) loose   (b) killer   dogs threatening them on school playgrounds, too. Keep your   (a) blood-thirsty beasts   (b) animals   tied up, or we will report them.

Which word is most emotional or "loaded," (a) or (b)?

____ 14. (a) vicious   (b) stray

____ 15. (a) loose   (b) killer

____ 16. (a) bloodthirsty beasts   (b) animals

17. The author wants people to   (a) report loose dogs   (b) keep their dogs tied up   (c) watch out for dangerous animals

GAS SHORTAGE

Drivers' licenses should not be given until age 20. There is no reason for kids younger than that to have licenses. Gasoline is needed for more important things than teenagers' social life. If we passed a law to change the legal driving age to 20, we would save millions of gallons of gas each year. When it is time to vote, vote yes to change the law.

18. What is the writer trying to get you to do?   (a) save gas   (b) vote to require teenagers to save gasoline   (c) limit driving to those persons 20 or older

19. If you want to limit driving to persons over 20, you must   (a) vote against the law   (b) vote for a change in the law   (c) vote to change gasoline rationing

V.   FIREWORKS

①There was a bang, and the rocket streaked high overhead.②Then it exploded and opened across the night sky like a huge umbrella.③Green, blue, gold, and white fireworks danced across the sky like jewels in a black tray.④Then another rocket jumped skyward and another.⑤The children laughed and clapped their hands.⑥It was better than a hundred birthdays all at once.

There are three similes in this paragraph. Write the number of the sentence and what the author uses as a comparison.

20. Sentence number ___ compares a rocket burst to _____.

21. Sentence number ___ compares the fireworks to _____.

22. Sentence number ___ compares the event to _____.

VI.   LIFESAVER

His brother jumped into the water while George stood on their makeshift diving board waiting for him to surface. Seconds went by. George began to worry. It was too long. More time. George knew it was too long. Then he saw his brother's back breaking the surface, but he was not swimming. He just floated motionless, and he was not moving. George jumped in feet first and swam toward his brother's floating body. He swam as fast as he could. As last he reached the spot.

23. Of the two paragraphs, FIREWORKS and LIFESAVER, which one uses the longest sentence?

   _____

24. Which of the two paragraphs has more long words (words of three or more syllables)?

   _____

25. Which one uses more figures of speech? _____

HOW DID YOU DO?

There is a total of 25 points on this test. Section I has 5 points; Section II has 2 points; Section III has 6 points; Section IV has 6 points; Section V has 3 points; and Section VI has 3 points.

Number right

23—25	Excellent
21—22	Good
17—20	Fair
16—0	Unsatisfactory

Answer Keys to Mastery Test

Section I

1. (b) Anne Benton
2. (a) Jessie Anderson
3. (c) Marty Jensen
4. (a) Jessie Anderson
5. (c) Marty Jensen

Section II

6. Sentence 1
7. Sentence 7

Section III

8. No
9. (a) visual images
10. (a) hopeful
11. Yes
12. (b) sound images
13. (b) fearful

Section IV

14. (a) vicious
15. (b) killer
16. (a) bloodthirsty beasts
17. (b) keep their dogs tied up
18. (c) limit driving to those over 20
19. (b) vote for a change in the law

Section V

20. Sentence 2 umbrella
21. Sentence 3 jewels in a black tray
22. Sentence 6 a hundred birthdays

Section VI

23. Lifesaver
24. Fireworks
25. Fireworks

SCORE SHEET

Kit VI   Critical Reading

STUDENT'S NAME:

PERCENTAGE CORRECT

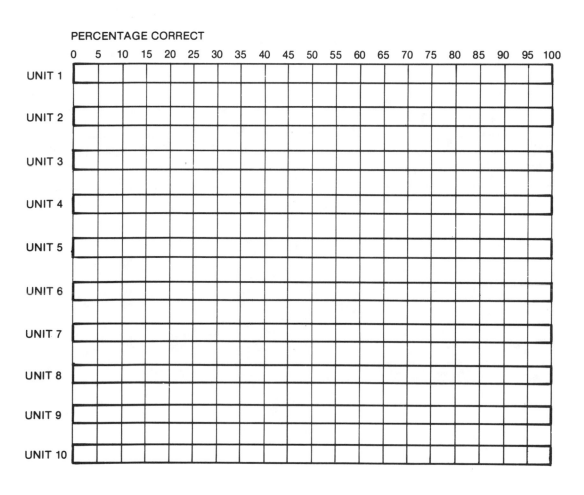